Hygge Home Habits

The Art of Nordic Simplicity and Coziness

Preface

Do you want to ease the stress in your life?

Learn how to relax?

Do you love being cozy and comfortable?

In that case, Hygge is for you.

Pronounced "Hoo-ga," Hygge is the ultimate Scandinavian way of life, a way of promoting coziness and contentment in your life. Scandinavians believe that the cozier you are, the better you feel; how you achieve that is up to you. It could be a relaxing cup of tea, wearing a pair of warm, comfy slippers, or wrapped up in a cozy blanket on the couch while the snow falls outside. In short, it's anything that makes you feel cozy and relaxed. And why you do it isn't important; it's the feeling it creates in you.

This book will take you through everything you need to know about bringing Hygge into your life. It will tell you how to adapt to a Hygge lifestyle, even if you don't have cold winters and short days where you live. All that's important is focusing on what makes you happy, relaxed, and less stressed.

There is no right or wrong time to start practicing Hygge in your life, but the sooner you start, the quicker you will feel more relaxed about your life, which can benefit you in many ways.

Table of Contents

Introduction

"Take your time getting dressed this morning; read a book, make yourself some breakfast. The world can wait." – Whitney Nobis.

There's a good reason why the Scandinavian countries, particularly Denmark, are among the happiest worldwide. That reason is called Hygge. Hygge, or "hoo-ga," is a Scandinavian concept mostly practiced in Denmark and Norway, and it revolves around comfort and coziness. Over the last few years, it has become one of the most popular lifestyles worldwide, but what is it? How can being comfortable and cozy benefit you?

Let's find out.

What Is Hygge?

The closest translation to Hygge is "cozy." It is a Scandinavian noun used to describe a feeling of warmth, coziness, and well-being. But don't make the mistake of thinking it is purely a trend. Hygge is a way of life. It's mindfulness and self-care at its best, a way to alleviate stress and make you feel so much better about yourself and your life, even when the weather is bad enough to make you feel down.

It is about being soothed, living in the moment, and expressing gratitude for everything, even the smallest things, that create joy and happiness in your life.

You can do Hygge alone – think of a snowy evening, curled up by the fire with a cup of hot cocoa – or do it with others – friends, family, anyone you enjoy being with. And while it is a way of life, it's also about you making the opportunities, creating the conditions for you to do it, even if it's only 10 minutes a day.

The practice of Hygge is important at all times, but even more so when you are facing difficult or stressful times. It can help you disconnect yourself from your worries, relax, and enjoy a few moments of calm.

Mindfulness and Self-Care

Don't think of Hygge as something you only do in the winter. Although it is a big part of Scandinavian life in the winters, when they only get a few hours of daylight, it should be a part of your everyday life, no matter what time of year or what the weather is like in your region. It's not just about snuggling down by the fire on a cold night. It's not about what your house or clothes look like or the food you eat. It's about your state of mind.

It's about taking time for yourself. It's about practicing mindfulness and gratitude and spending time alone or with people who make you happy. In short, it's about living joyfully and intentionally.

The Mental Health Benefits

Suggesting that you should light a candle and drink a cup of cocoa to relieve depression or major stresses in your life would be stupid; it takes much more than that. Hygge is about good mental health, about doing things you know help you feel better about yourself and life. It's about relieving your mind from daily worries and bringing a sense of calm. Some of the mental health benefits you can enjoy from practicing Hygge are:

- **Gratitude:** It's well-known that gratitude and good mental health go together. While you could keep a gratitude journal to help you document your journey and right down all you are grateful for, Hygge will also help you feel grateful for things in your life, and that's because Hygge is based on the simple pleasures in life.

- **Self-Care:** Hygge is about taking time for yourself, and you can do this in many ways. It could just be five minutes sitting by yourself, a few hours at the spa, or an entire evening of self-care. Some people make up self-soothing kits containing calming music, scented candles, cozy slippers and blankets, cushions, and anything else that makes you feel calm.

- **Mindfulness:** This is one of the more helpful parts of Hygge because it helps you learn to be in the moment and make the most of it. It's about focusing on what's around you and getting pleasure from the here and now.

- **Reduced Stress:** Managing stress is an important part of life – everyone experiences it at some time, some more than others. Hygge teaches you to reduce your stress by allowing yourself to take a break, focus on yourself, your surroundings, and your senses, and do things that bring you joy.

- **Lower Anxiety:** By practicing Hygge, you introduce calm into your life, which can help your anxiety levels reduce. In turn, this can help you feel better about yourself and more secure, and your anxiety levels will reduce.

- **Better Connections:** Hygge is also about creating great connections. You might opt to meet a couple of close friends for coffee in your favorite café or invite them over for a cozy meal. Whatever makes you feel good and deepen those connections, but steer clear of talking about anything controversial!

- **Happiness:** Every one of the benefits above leads to you feeling happier and more contented with life, which makes you feel better about yourself.

Hygge may be practiced more in the winter, but it should be followed all year round. It's a fantastic way to help you slow down, take notice of what's around you, and take time for yourself. Anyone can do it; just find things that bring you pleasure daily and do them – your life will be much better for it.

Let's dive into the specifics of Hygge and find out how you can turn your life around with this simple practice.

Chapter 1

Hygge Your House

"There is nothing like staying at home for real comfort"
– Jane Austen

How often do you look around your house and wonder how to make it feel warm and cozy? The answer could lie in Hygge, a Scandinavian lifestyle that is fast becoming popular the world over. This chapter will walk you through the Hygge principles and provide a practical guide on using Hygge in your home to make it calm, cozy, and peaceful.

The Hygge Lifestyle

Hygge focuses on simplicity, coziness, and happiness. It means making your home an uncluttered, peaceful place to relax and enjoy time alone or with your friends and family. It's about creating somewhere safe to relax and unwind from the stresses of life.

One of the biggest focuses of Hygge is the home – it should be inviting and warm. When you set your home up the right way, the colder seasons become easier to enjoy, and your health and happiness soar. Using the right décor is a significant part of this, and the rest of this chapter is devoted to giving you tips on achieving the perfect hygge home.

Hygge décor isn't just about aesthetics; it's about embracing well-being, warmth, and the simple things in life that bring you pleasure, exactly how the Scandinavians live. Below, you can read about the principles you should follow to create the right soul-nurturing atmosphere:

Embrace Nature:

This is one of the most important aspects. Integrating natural elements into your home can help you create a welcoming space, creating a connection to nature that can boost your health and well-being. Choosing neutral, warm colors and natural textures, like wool and wood, can help you create a comfortable, cozy, inviting space.

Here are some tips on using natural elements:
- Create a focal point in the heart of your home.
- Have a centerpiece of candles.

- Have warm lamps scattered strategically around the room.
- Over your furniture with warm, cozy cushions and blankets.
- Use acorns, branches, dried flower arrangements, and pinecones to Hygge your home in a unique way.
- Choose furniture made from natural wood – vintage is better than new – to create a cozy atmosphere.

When you use nature, you add texture and warmth while creating a sustainable, eco-friendly space.

Warm Colors and Textures:

Using the right color palette is critical to creating the right atmosphere. Choose warm, neutral colors and textures:

- Beige and cream should be the main colors.
- Don't use overwhelming, bright colors.
- Use different textures to add interest and depth – wood, wool, soft fabrics, etc.

Textures are just as important and a great way of making a minimalist design look interesting. Think about using rustic wood, sherpa throws, and warm knit blankets.

Mixing up a few different textures makes your home warm, inviting, and visually appealing.

While your color palette should be mostly neutral, it must be uplifting and tranquil, so choose those colors that make you feel good and evoke happiness, comfort, and warmth in your life.

Use Soft Lighting:

Soft lighting is one of the best ways to create an inviting, warm, and cozy atmosphere. You can achieve this by:

- Having candles lit around the room.
- Use subtle fairy lights to add a warm touch.
- Change your light bulbs to warm-light ones.
- Put a warm-light lamp near your favorite chair or sofa to make you feel cozy.

You can also add more natural light to your home by:

- Open your curtains.
- Place mirrors on the walls opposite your windows, creating the illusion of double the natural light.
- Choose orange-tinted lights rather than blue.
- Place lamps around the coziest parts of the room.
- Use electric candles rather than real ones if you

have pets and children – they are much safer. You should also choose some pieces of music that soothe and relax you and have them playing softly in the background. Alternatively, play white noise – the sounds of a fire crackling in the hearth, for example. You can also have a pot of natural ingredients simmering on the stove or essential oils in a diffuser with a warm scent.

Create Some Cozy Spaces:
These are the heart of your hygge home. It could be something as simple as a little reading nook, a cozy seating area, or creating a cozy bedroom. No matter what it is, it must be decorated in the right way to create that cozy feeling.

- Use cozy furniture – a comfortable loveseat or chair, for example – and add throws and cushions. Place it near a warm, soft-light lamp or a window, and add a small side table.
- Reuse natural items, so long as they are neutral colors, such as hamper baskets made from natural materials.
- Have some books on display to make the area more inviting.

Creating cozy corners in your home provides the ideal way to unwind and enjoy the atmosphere, but you must add a few personal touches, too:

- Set up a tray on your little side table and fill it with some of your favorite things – a soy candle, miniature photos of your loved ones, or a serving bowl with your favorite sweets or cookies.
- Add framed art or photos that make you happy.
- Add a throw or cushion in your favorite patterns or colors.
- Display souvenirs that make you happy.

Anything that makes you feel happy and relaxed will make your cozy space special.

Sentimental and Personal Items:

The personal touch is the best way to make your hygge décor unique. Adding sentimental items, photos, vintage pieces you inherited, and anything meaningful to you can make your space emotionally inviting and help you tell your story. Some ideas are:

- A teapot you inherited from your gran
- A beautiful piece of art handed down through your family
- Cherished family photos

These can bring you memories of happy times while adding a touch of history. You can also add a touch of the vintage to your home with items that have visual appeal:

- Old metal signs
- Rustic chalkboards
- Banners
- Garlands
- Silhouettes

These give your space character and charm and act as conversation subjects when you share your space with others.

Declutter and Simplify:

This is perhaps the most important part of Hygge: freeing your home of clutter to create a peaceful space. Simplicity is key, allowing you to focus on what really matters and create the perfect space for happiness and relaxation.

To do this, you must go through everything in your home, room by room, and only keep what makes you happy. This can be one of the most liberating things you will ever do, as it allows you to get rid of things you don't need and keep only what is truly important to you. Making your space simple and clutter-free will help you feel calmer and happier, enjoying the real benefits of Hygge and contributing to a happier life.

Seasonal Décor:

Using seasonal décor helps you keep your home inviting and cozy throughout the year, not just in the colder seasons. Throws in seasonal colors, centerpieces made from natural seasonal items, and candles scented to match the season all help create an ever-evolving, welcoming atmosphere, no matter the time of year.

In the colder months, you could use cushions in warm tones, faux-fur throws, and candles scented with pine, cinnamon, or chocolate to create the right atmosphere that makes you feel warm and cozy. Conversely, in the warmer months, you could use lighter throws made from natural materials, fresh flowers and greenery, and candles with lighter floral scents.

When you embrace the seasons, your home stays fresh while helping to nurture your happiness and peace within yourself.

Spend Time with Your Loved Ones:

The hygge lifestyle is about peace and reducing stress in your life, but it's also about spending time with the people who really matter to you. It's about creating new memories that none of you will ever forget. Your home should be designed to give you space for alone time while encouraging togetherness. That could be a cozy area with comfy seating and a coffee table or dining table arrangement that allows you all to enjoy your meals in a way that brings you together.

Hygge isn't just about your physical surroundings. It's also about the emotions and experiences that bring you all together, and making time to be with your loved ones in a warm, cozy environment is the best way to truly embrace the hygge lifestyle.

How to Integrate Hygge into Your Everyday Life

The only way to embrace Hygge to its fullest is to ensure its principles are a part of your daily life. Do this by:

- Practicing gratitude and mindfulness.
- Enjoy the simple things in life that bring you pleasure.
- Make your home a cozy place all year round.

Doing these things daily can bring Hygge into your life and experience the immense benefits of a healthier, happier life.

Set some time aside every day to do things that help you relax and make you happy. This could be sitting down to enjoy your favorite drink, reading a book, or taking a stroll through nature. Put the effort in to be present in the moment and revel in the little pleasures life throws your way.

Create the perfect, fulfilling, happy life that makes you feel better physically, emotionally, and mentally by embracing Hygge to its fullest.

Chapter 2

Hygge Together

"Everyone of us needs to show how much we care for each other and, in the process, care for ourselves."
– Princess Diana.

Humans are social creatures, always looking for connections, not just for survival but to help them evolve and thrive. Every person has a unique relationship with themselves but also needs relationships with others, which should help them lead a happy, fulfilled life.

Today, everyone lives a busy, fast-paced life, heavily reliant on the digital, connected world that has only served to create huge chasms in human relationships. Let's say it's your best friend's birthday. Do you wish her a happy birthday via her social media page, or pick up the phone and talk to her? Which one offers the most value and brings the most joy?

Making time to see people, to connect with them, is an important hygge concept. In your busy rush through life, you don't take time to stop, to notice things around you, and, more importantly, to deepen your connections with the important people in your life. When you do stop and take the time to be in the moment and appreciate everything and everyone around you, it can bring a real sense of calm and belonging to your life.

When you can learn to be in the moment and appreciate life for yourself, you'll find connecting with those around you much easier, gaining enrichment and happiness you may never have thought possible. That's what Hygge is all about, urging you to deepen and cherish relationships with friends and family.

Using Hygge to Build Healthy Relationships

The hygge principles to building great relationships are:

Communication:

Open, honest communication is important in forming healthy relationships and helping them grow and deepen. Hygge is about being present, slowing down, and taking time for yourself and others.

The best way to Communicate effectively with the other people in your life is to learn to push distractions aside and give them your full attention. This creates a comfortable space for you to be in and helps you deepen your connections, which leads to much stronger Hygge feelings.

Effective communication requires you to:

- Remove distractions so you can get more involved in the communication – that means switching off your phone!
- Do not rush the conversation; take the time to get fully involved.
- Do not jump in when someone else is talking; let them finish first.
- Be fully open to the conversation.
- Disagree when the need arises, but never just for the sake of it.
- Participate in the two-way street of conversation.
- Be mindful when you listen. Listening attentively helps you feel safe and deepens the conversational quality.

Connection:

The internet has made connectivity so much easier but not in the best way, and certainly not in the hygge way. The internet certainly allows you to build connections, but not physical ones. True Hygge requires you to spend time with your loved ones and have real conversations, not digital ones.

There are several ways you can create those connections and enter into the spirit of Hygge:

- Throw a potluck dinner and invite your nearest and dearest.
- Throw game or movie nights.
- Arrange BBQs, picnics, campfire get-togethers, or road trips with others.
- Host an online party if your friends and family are far away, but do it over video so you can all see each other.

Cooperation:

Finally, cooperation is important in a hygge lifestyle. It's about being there for each other, helping when needed, and getting involved. Basically, the overriding principle of Hygge is togetherness. Some of the ways you can get involved are:

- Volunteer to work as part of a team – pet rescues, hosting local events, and so on.
- Taking part in group activities.
- Learning to recognize when you need help and asking for it. It could be as simple as asking your family to get involved in helping you with

a cookout or catering a party to asking for help to get you through a tough time. When you ask for help, it encourages trust, togetherness, safety, and comfort.

These are just some ways you can bring Hygge into your relationships. It is all about being together, spending time with those you love, and deepening your connections. It's about being present, not just in the moment, but for your loved ones. It's about making them an important part of your life and making time to be together physically. Think about it – when did you last sit down with your friends or family and engage in real conversation? You might be shocked at the answer, so now's the time to start getting involved and strengthening those relationships.

Chapter 3

Hygge Your Dress Sense

"I like canceled plans. And empty bookstores. I like rainy days and thunderstorms. And quiet coffee shops. I like messy beds and over-worn pajamas. Most of all, I like the small joys that a simple life brings." – Unknown.

In recent years, Scandinavian fashion has taken a real foothold in other countries, and that's because it is so simple while embodying quality and fashion. Scandinavians bring Hygge into their lives in the way they dress, and there are several ways you can achieve this, no matter where you live:

- **Wear Layers:** Because Hygge is mainly a cold-weather concept, wearing layers helps you stay warm while looking stylish. Soft sweaters should be layered with cozy cardigans, scarves, and any other cozy clothing that helps you achieve the right look. Wearing layers means you can remove a piece of clothing if the temperature increases or add another layer if it gets colder. Using different materials and textures can also keep things interesting. For example, you could wear a pair of tighter-fitting jeans with a large, chunky sweater or a thinner sweater and a chunky cardigan. Add a warm scarf and a hat, and you've got your look for the day.

- **Keep Things Neutral:** Try to stick to neutral, pastel, or earth-toned colors. Not only do they look smart and stylish, but it's also easier to mix and match your look. These are calming colors that create a cozy look, and they also ensure your wardrobe is more cohesive.

- **Focus on Comfort:** Hygge fashion is about wearing clothes that make you feel cozy and comfortable. Think of shearling, knitted wear, and faux fur brought together in comfortable layers. Soft cardigans help you feel comfortable while achieving a laid-back casual look, while chunky socks, warm boots, and shoes lined with shearling bring comfort. That doesn't mean you can just throw on any old clothing or live in your favorite leggings and sweaters all the time. Take the time to dress conscientiously and intentionally while staying comfortable.

- **Quality, Not Quantity:** Having a huge wardrobe stuffed with clothes goes against the Hygge principles of simplicity and clutter-free. Part of living a hygge lifestyle means only keeping what makes you happy, so invest in a few higher quality pieces and keep them in neutral colors that you can easily mix and match to create different looks.

- **Don't Forget the Coat:** These should be warm and comfy, so in the winter, think puffer coats, faux fur, or even long chunky cardigans that keep you warm while being stylish. Have a look in vintage stores; you might find the perfect coat to help you create that look. And don't forget warm chunky socks, hats, mittens, and scarves to complete your look.

- **Think Sustainability:** Second-hand plays a big part in Hygge, giving pre-loved, good-condition clothing a second chance at life instead of being sent to the landfill. Don't be afraid to scour the second-hand shops to find that perfect piece of clothing, knowing that you are embracing the Hygge lifestyle and practicing sustainability.

- **Keep Nature in Mind:** Choose clothing made from natural fibers and textures rather than synthetic ones. This could be wool, cotton, or linen, all of which are breathable and keep you cool (linen and cotton) or warm (wool) – something synthetic fabrics fail to do. You can also bring nature into your colors, using neutral, natural colors and mixing them to create an amazing hygge look.

Hygge goes way beyond fashion, but dressing the part helps you feel happier, warmer, and more comfortable. Don't just dress for going out. Bring Hygge fashion into every aspect of your life, be it a fashionable party, a get-together with your friends, or an evening spent by the fire with a good book and cup of cocoa.

Everyone has an inner Hygge voice; you just need to learn to listen to yours.

Chapter 4

Hygge-ify Your Diet

"When you recover or discover something that nourishes your soul and brings joy, care enough about yourself to make room for it in your life." – Jean Shinoda Bolen.

As more and more people adopt the hygge lifestyle, their attention turns to creating a warm, cozy living space. But Hygge isn't a style – it's a feeling, which means you can bring it into every part of your life, including your diet. Here's how you can gain immense joy from what you eat every day:

Be Mindful:

This applies to how and where you eat. Hygge nutrition isn't just about what you eat but also about how you eat it. Most people lead such busy lives that they eat on the go or as they sit mindlessly in front of the TV at night. Mealtimes are meant to be a time for you to slow down, pause your busy lifestyle, and enjoy what you eat and the company you are in. Lighting a few candles, playing soft music, and using good silverware can turn the simplest meals into something special.

Buy some good tealights and arrange them throughout your space. Lay faux fur or soft throws over your dining chairs, and add a centerpiece made from something natural, like flowers, to your dining table – not so big that you can't see over it, though.

Setting up your dining space mindfully will ensure more enjoyment from your meal, whether a gourmet meal or something simple. If you prefer to eat in front of the TV, you can Hygge the space with comfy blankets and cushions on your sofa or chairs and settle down to watch something that helps you unwind.

Eat Seasonal Foods:

Each season brings its own food. You might have new potatoes and the first asparagus shoots in the spring, while summer brings plump, sweet berries. The pumpkins come in the fall, while winter means onions, carrots, garlic, peas, and rhubarb. Of course, this depends on your region and climate, but you should eat seasonal produce wherever possible. It's cheaper, tastier, and more eco-friendly, cutting the carbon footprint immensely, especially if you eat local foods. You also feed your body the nutrition it needs all year round and align with nature. Head to a farmers market near you or grow your own if you have the space and time. In fact, growing your own garden, even a small one, can help you embrace Hygge as it lets you embrace nature.

Eat Local Foods:

Seasonal is one thing, but eating locally-produced foods is even better. Not only are your foods fresher, but it also builds a connection with your local community, an important Hygge concept. Again, what you can eat depends on your local region, but as a rule, you should try to eat as much local, seasonal, fresh food as possible.

For example, if you live in a coastal region, the seafood caught there will be incredibly fresh, much more so than what you can buy in a grocery store. If you live in a region with abundant fruit orchards, you won't have trouble buying the freshest fruits. Again, head to farmer's markets and farm-to-table stores to do your shopping.

Don't Plan Ahead Too Much:

For most people, bulk shopping and meal prepping is the norm but when you plan too far ahead, you aren't following Hygge. You eat far less fresh, seasonal food this way and aren't listening to what your body wants and what you would enjoy eating. Let's say you wake up feeling like you could eat a pasta dish made with fresh tomatoes for dinner. Heading to the market and buying fresh ingredients is far more satisfying than pulling a pre-made meal out of the freezer. And doing less shopping in one go means you'll buy fresher foods more often and you can vary your diet significantly. For example, when you head to the fish market, you could opt for the catch of the day rather than that piece of salmon you always buy. And your fruits, veggies, and salads will be crisper, fresher and tastier.

Take the Time for Kaffe:

Can you think back to the last time you sat down to enjoy a cup of coffee without being in a rush or sitting in front of your computer? Have you ever made a pot of fresh coffee and invited your best friends for an enjoyable time-out? That's where "kaffe" comes in. Yes, the word literally means "coffee" but in hygge terms, it is a culture. When you follow a hygge lifestyle, you don't just down your coffee just to give you a shot of energy for the day. You sit and you enjoy every sip you take. You can do this by yourself, but it's even better when you do it with family or friends.

Make time for kaffe in your daily schedule. You can take a little extra time over your morning coffee, join your friends in a local café, or even invite your family for coffee in the afternoon or evening. Even if you head to the local coffee shop, take someone with you to foster that sense of togetherness and community.

Feed Your Sweet Tooth:

You won't find many books that tell you to enjoy eating sugary foods, but denying yourself takes some of the pleasure out of life. Think of spending a cold afternoon in a warm, cozy café with your friends, with a cup of coffee or hot chocolate and a freshly baked cookie. Or an evening in front of the fire with some friends and a delicious chocolate cake. Desserts are a big part of the Scandinavian lifestyle, but enjoying them responsibly is key. If you mindlessly binge on a pile of candy or plow through a pint of ice cream, you won't be experiencing the hygge part. Take your time. Indulge yourself now and then, and take pleasure from eating something sweet on occasion, but don't feed a sugar addiction. You could try your hand at baking your favorite cookies, ones that evoke happy memories, and invite your friends or neighbors over to enjoy them with you. And don't forget the kaffe!

How to Host a Delicious Hygge Gathering

Winter is the best time of year for Hygge, mainly because the weather is extremely cold in Denmark and other Scandinavian countries, and the night skies last around 17 hours. It's the perfect time of year to gather your friends and family and hold a wonderful Hygge evening. Here are some tips to help you:

Keep It Small

Don't fill your house with people. Hygge gatherings are intimate, with a few special people who can gather and chat without struggling to be heard over masses of people. Invite people who get on well together and a few others you know who you might want your family and friends to get to know.

Serve Comfort Food:

You want food you can prepare easily (or get everyone else to help you prepare), and that brings comfort and happiness to your guests. Think quiche, casseroles made with local and seasonal ingredients, and delicious desserts. You could even prepare a series of different fondues – cheese, broth, chocolate, etc., as these are a wonderful way for everyone to gather around and chat while enjoying a leisurely evening.

Serve Warming Drinks:

The drink is as important as the food at a get-together and on a cold evening, and what better way to hydrate your guests than with mulled wine, hot chocolate, apple cider, and non-alcoholic toddies for those who don't drink?

Have Candles Everywhere:

If you have an open fire, light it so it crackles merrily away in the background, but if you don't, consider lighting some tall pillar candles to provide a similar warm effect. Use scented candles dotted around to evoke seasonal smells, and have plenty of tealights dotted around, too. You can use electric or battery candles if you prefer, as these are much safer while still giving the same effect.

Aim for simple, understated lighting that provides enough light but not too much. Layer your lighting in levels, using wall sconces, table lamps, portrait lights, etc., but no bright overhead lights. These will kill off the mood quicker than anything.

Other Ways to Create the Right Hygge Feeling:

- **Music:** Create a suitable playlist of soft music to play in the background. It must be pleasant but not loud.

- **Conversation:** If some of your guests are strangers to the others, you'll need to think of some conversation starters. You may not need them – if you have the right bunch of guests, they'll mingle and chat as though they all know one another. You could also kick things off with a quiz or a few games to help everyone feel at home and comfortable.

- **Clothes:** You could host a themed/fancy party and request that your guests dress up in their cocktail finery, but that's not the Hygge way. Your guests must feel comfortable, not self-conscious, so tell them to wear whatever they want, whatever they feel the most cozy wearing, even if it's fleecy leggings, chunky socks, and a sloppy big sweater.

You could also have a basket of slippers, socks, and piles of cozy blankets to help your friends feel more settled and cozy for the evening ahead.

Whatever you do, don't put yourself under pressure to make the evening just right. Your guests will do that for you, so just provide the right food and atmosphere and let them do the rest.

Chapter 5

Hygge for the Holiday Season

"Winter is the time for comfort, for good food and warmth, for the touch of a friendly hand, and for a talk beside the fire: it is time for home."
– Edith Sitwell.

Are you looking forward to the holiday season or dreading it because it's always so hard to prep for and always feels forced? If it's the latter, you're not doing it right. You need to bring some hygge to your holiday season and make it what you've always wanted it to be. Here are some ideas on how to Hygge your holiday season and make it a time to look forward to with joy and happiness.

Arrange a Get-Together:
This might be what causes you the most stress – having friends and family over for the holidays and spending all your time worrying about getting everything right. It shouldn't be that way. You don't have to have everyone

together in your home at the same time; the holiday season offers plenty of opportunities for you to get together with others, so think about hosting smaller groups of people at different times – and pick your guests carefully.

Above all, don't stress about it. A Hygge party should be friendly and relaxed, which is why potlucks and fondue parties work so well.

Cut Your Own Tree:
Get together with your family or friends, head to a tree farm, and choose your own tree. Part of the hygge lifestyle is to use natural products where possible – you won't see many synthetic holiday trees in Denmark! If you have the space, why not grow your own tree and chop it down as a family? It will take all of you to do it together, and it is a real bonding experience.

Light Candles:
Candles are a big thing in the holiday season, all day and all night. They are the essence of Christmas and most Scandinavian families will have a large candle or a calendar candle that they allow to burn down without putting it out. These typically burn all day and are usually blown out the next morning at breakfast by someone in

the family – usually a child, but if you don't have any, do it yourself. This is a cozy way of symbolizing that Christmas is one day nearer.

Warm Lighting:

Fill your home with warm, soft lights to enhance your space and make it look more cozy. Fairly lights are an excellent choice this time of year, and if you want to be really sustainable and eco-conscious, use solar-powered lights. Of course, in countries with little daylight, these won't work, but they will in other parts of the world where days are much longer. If you have an open fireplace or even a gas or electric fire that looks like it has real flames, get it going – these are a great way to make the atmosphere cozy and warm.

Sing Around Your Tree:

This is a wonderful Hygge tradition, gathering your family and friends together, lighting the tree (traditionally, candles are used, but that may not always be safe), and dancing around the tree while singing songs – all holding hands. This is traditionally done before presents are opened, and Scandinavian kids absolutely love it – you will, too.

Bake and Play:

Get your friends and family involved in baking and decorating holiday cookies, and play lots of games together. Forget the TV – there's not usually much on over the holidays, anyway – and immerse yourself in each other's company. Everyone should be involved in the baking, from getting the ingredients together to making the dough, baking the cookies, and especially decorating them. Everyone knows they are included, creating a wonderful, fun atmosphere of togetherness and peace.

Make Holiday Ornaments:

Another tradition is that everyone gets together and makes ornaments for the tree. Usually, these are made from salt dough, baked, decorated, and hung on the tree, and everyone gets to make their own personal ones. It's a great tradition that ensures everyone is involved from start to finish.

Involve Everyone in the Food:

Everyone should be involved in the holiday food, no matter who hosts the get-together. Cook foods people find comforting, like turkey or ham, chili, stew, fruit pies, cookies, and other foods that people love at that time of the year. All these give off amazing scents and a warmth that makes everyone feel cozy. Give everyone a job to do and gather in the kitchen to prepare a feast that will bring you all together.

What Not to Do

If you want a Hygge holiday, there are some things you must avoid when you get together with your friends and family. You should not:

- Talk about politics or any other potentially controversial subject.
- Brag about things.
- Talk down about others.
- Be negative in any way.
- Spend all your time on your phone or tablet or watching TV.

These are all things that will sink the mood quickly, so get a conversation started about happy things, start singing, get involved in helping with preparation, leave your phones to one side, and be present in the moment. Concentrate on the people you share your holidays with and express gratitude and thankfulness for them.

7 Steps to a Hygge Holiday

Creating the perfect hygge holiday means following the steps taken by the Scandinavians, and those steps are:

1. Be Present

Hygge's roots lie in mindfulness, awareness, and enjoying the small pleasures in life. That means slowing down and being more present is important. Sadly, the holiday season tends to make most of us feel the opposite way, simply because there's so much to do that it ends up being the most stressful time of the year.

You can change that with a few simple steps. Start by sitting down and remembering what the holiday season is about. Make time to be with your friends and family instead of just buying gifts. Get together to wrap your gifts and, just for once, let the cleaning slide. It will still be there later.

Sit at your window and watch the snow falling while you wrap your hands around a hot drink. Take your kids sledding, or get together with some friends and go sledding with them.

Even if you live somewhere warm, you can still practice Hygge. Create opportunities to get together and enjoy company, food, wine, and days out, and leave your phones alone while you do it.

This will surely get you in the hygge mood, and the rest will follow easily.

Time Is More Important Than Gifts

Yes, it's nice to get gifts, be they practical or otherwise. but spending time together is far more important. Holiday Hygge is all about intimacy, togetherness, and connections – the gifts are just a nice afterthought. Yet, many people spend too much time worrying about and looking for the right gifts for people and not enough time actually being with the people they are buying for. Yes, buy your friends and family gifts, but make sure you all spend time together over the holidays – it's far more enriching than any gift, no matter the cost or practicality of it.

Create a Hygge Holiday Space

That doesn't mean you have to go out and empty the shops of candles or follow the latest Pinterest or Instagram holiday decorating guides. Holiday Hygge isn't about looks. It's about creating a calm, peaceful space that reflects the feelings you want to invoke in yourself. Soft lighting, candles, and the minimum amount of decorations, preferably made from natural materials, are all that's needed to create the perfect hygge space. Too many people clutter their homes with decorations over the holiday season. Forget that and go for minimal and calming.

Scandinavian Christmas Lasts at Least One Week

For most people, Christmas is just two days. Maybe that's because you have to go back to work, but it doesn't mean you can't have a longer holiday season. Danish Christmas starts on the 23rd of December (officially, anyway), but it will continue into the New Year. Traditionally, extended families get together, go to Mass, and then celebrate with a large meal, while Christmas Day is kept for smaller gatherings and children. The shops don't open for the whole week and everyone gets to celebrate.

In today's world, people would be horrified if the shops closed down for a week, but you can still make time for a longer Hygge holiday by doing as much as possible before the start of Christmas, giving you time to be present, spend time with loved ones, and be spontaneous.

Create Your Own Traditions

Holiday Hygge is also about traditions, but you don't have to follow the tried and tested ones. Because spontaneity is a big part of things, try to create your own. It could be family gatherings to buy, chop, and decorate your tree, hang stockings on Christmas Eve, or bake holiday cookies. Whatever it is, it should be something that has personal meaning to everyone involved and that makes your holiday season unique.

Scandinavian families gather to decorate their trees and call it "little Christmas." They've always done it and will continue to do it, but you can do whatever makes Christmas special for you.

Serve Up a Feast

One of the truly great things about a Scandinavian Christmas is their food – they don't hold back! A traditional holiday meal is an elaborate Smorgasbord of delicious foods for everyone to enjoy. All restaurants close, and everyone joins their family and friends for intimate gatherings at home around a table laden with food. And we can't forget the drink. Traditional drinks are Akvavit and beer, but you can serve whatever makes you happy. Just don't forget to use the good glasses!

Get Outside

There's nothing like a bit of fresh air, even when it's freezing cold outside. Scandinavian families are all quite happy to go outside in sub-zero weather and play together in the snow, but many other cultures won't do it. It's time to ditch the centrally heated house for some crisp, clean air that wakes the senses, pushes anxiety out of the window, and helps you calm down. Gather your friends and family and head out for a snowball fight, sledding, or just a walk in nature. You won't regret it. Hygge your holidays in a way that makes sense to you, helps you feel the calm and peace you want, and brings you all together to enjoy the season in harmony. And don't forget to start a few new traditions of your own.

Chapter 6

Three Steps to Real Hygge Event

"Almost everything will work again if you unplug it for a few minutes, including you." – Anne Lamott.

In the truest sense of the word, Hygge is about feeling safe, but it's also about being present. It's not just about having candles everywhere, sipping mugs of hot chocolate, and eating your favorite foods. These are the things that everyone seems to focus on when they think of Hygge, but there's far more to it.

The most important Hygge elements are the intangible ones. Think about the last time you went out for a nice meal with a loved one in a fancy restaurant, with lovely wine and romantic candles. Was that Hygge? Most likely not because, although you were there, you probably weren't truly present in the moment. A prerequisite to Hygge is a feeling of safety and disconnection from all the worries of the world while being connected to yourself and those around you.

You don't have to go full Hygge right from the start. Start small with a Hygge event to help you and your loved ones connect. For your Hygge event to be authentic and to work for you, there are three essential steps:

The Hygge Oath

While spontaneity is one of the key elements, preparing for it is far from spontaneous. Everyone needs to be in the right mood, but what is that mood? First, you must plan Hygge ahead of time; it rarely happens without preparation. You can't just say, "Let's all get together and Hygge!"

Hygge is a very special part of your life, and everyone needs to know what to expect and when the hygge get-together will happen. Everyone should also know that they should take the Hygge oath when attending the get-together. It can be said silently, or you can all say it out loud together. But what is that oath? It could be the following, or you could write your own, so long as it meets the hygge requirements:

"I will respect the hygge rules, and I will not spoil things for me or the others."

Not only that, but you already know that planning something builds anticipation, which is positive and satisfying and creates the right atmosphere for your

Hygge event. So, whether this is just a one-off gathering or something that happens regularly, plan for it and make sure everyone is prepared.

Disconnection

Are you struggling with things at work? Kick them into touch. Got personal issues? The same. Kick all your anxieties, worries, and distractions into touch – you don't want anything to detract from enjoying your Hygge time, nor do you want anything to distract the others. This is a big, non-negotiable Hygge rule – leave your worries at the door.

Hygge is about feeling safe and being disconnected from negativity. It's about being positive and upbeat. Just one small spark of negativity can destroy the entire Hygge atmosphere for everyone, so the most important thing is to ensure that everyone involved knows the rules.

This includes switching off or muting phones, tablets, and any other device that can distract people – preferably, they should left in bags or another room, out of sight, out of mind. If you hold your Hygge event at home, the only electronic device allowed is a laptop, computer, or smart TV switched to YouTube with a video of a crackling fire playing. That will help warm the atmosphere and produce feel-good vibes.

Connection

Whoa! Connection? Isn't the idea of Hygge to be disconnected? Well, yes, but only from distractions. The real idea is to strengthen connections with what really matters – the people with you. This is why most hygge events are small and include only close family and friends, the people you really enjoy being with and want to connect with. If you don't know someone that well, you'll struggle to bond with them, which means you won't connect.

Togetherness is an absolute must, the most important Hygge element of all. Being present means you'll find it easier to connect with others, and the atmosphere will be friendly, happy, and full of joy.

This is why it is so important to do things together. Start your event by talking about good memories you've shared, even right back to your childhood. Trips you've been on, experiences you've shared, or anything that brings back good memories and makes you happy is allowed. Positivity has an amazing effect on how people feel; once one person starts sharing, others will follow. You can also play games, sing together, or do anything that involves togetherness and fun. Don't brag, and don't show off. Distractions aren't the only thing you should leave at the door – your ego must stay outside, too.

Helpful Hygge and Other Danish Vocabulary

"Be present in all things, and thankful for all things."
- Maya Angelou.

Following Hygge is one thing, but what about some of the hygge words you hear? What on earth do they mean? Hygge language is fun, and learning a few words and phrases can help you elevate your experience. And if you decide to head to Denmark, attempting their language will endear you to the people, and they'll go out of their way to help you.

Hygge Words and Phrases:

Hygge:

The obvious one to start with, the word "Hygge" comes from "hugga," a Norwegian word that means "to console" or "to comfort." It is also one of Danish culture's most defining concepts. Hygge relates to feeling contented, comforted, cozy, and well, and it's easily achieved with the simple pleasures in life. It's about creating an environment where you feel safe, a welcoming place where you and others can be themselves in comfort. Think of a crackling fire, candles flickering everywhere, warm, cozy throws and pillows, hot chocolate, and much laughter.

You can incorporate Hygge into any area of your life, be it your home, workplace, meals, or wardrobe. One of the most important ways is to get together with others, host fun days out, evening potlucks, game or movie nights, or anything that brings you and your loved ones together.

Hyggelig:

This adjective describes something as pleasant, cozy, or nice. For example:

- **En hyggelig aften:** means a cozy/pleasant/nice evening.
- **En hyggelig gammel mand:** a nice or pleasant old man.
- **Et hyggelig t(h) ekøkken:** a kitchen that's packed with hygge. You would say something like this after a lovely evening spent with a loved one or a group of close friends or family.

- **Det var hyggeligt:** means "it's been a pleasure."

At Hygge Sig:

This is a phrase that means to enjoy yourself in a hyggelig manner.

Hygger I jer:

Something you would say to your guests: "Are you all having a good time?"

De Hyggede Sig Rigtigt Meget I Sofaen:

This means "They enjoyed themselves on the sofa." This is merely a way of saying a gathering of people in a friend's home had a good time on the sofa, eating a meal, watching a movie, etc.

At Hygge:

Another verb, you can use it without adding "sig," but you cannot say "hyg" without adding "dig." However, if you say it without using the reflexive pronouns – "mig," "os," "dig," or "jer," it is informal. For example, "Nu skal vi rigtigt hygge!" means "Now, we are really going to have a great time!"

En Hygger:

This is a slang term for someone who enjoys "at high sig" or does a lot of hygging!

You can combine the word "hygge" with just about anything:

- **Aftenhygge:** an evening hygge
- **Sofahygge:** any hygge event that takes place on a sofa – eating, watching a movie, playing a game, and so on.

Other words you might want to learn are:

- **Hyggeslik:** hygge candy
- **Hyggesnak:** hygge talk
- **Hyggesludder:** hygge chat
- **Hyggethe:** hygge tea
- **Forårshygge:** spring hygge
- **Sommerhygge:** summer hygge
- **Efterårshygge:** autumn/fall hygge
- **Vinterhygge:** winter hygge
- **Familiehygge:** family hygge – applies when you get together with your family for a meal, a game, a movie night, or anything that brings you together and brings the hygge feeling to you all.
- **Filmhygge:** film hygge, when you or a group of family, friends, or even a pet gather to watch a movie.
- **Fødselsdagshygge**: birthday hygge, when you celebrate your birthday with your favorite

family or friends in a way that makes you feel good.

- **Sondagshygge:** Sunday hygge, when you have a relaxing day with friends or family. All shops close on this day, allowing everyone to spend time with their loved ones.

- **Bajerhygge/hyggebajar:** hygge with your favorite beer

- **Hyggebukser:** hygge pants – your favorite pants for wearing at home but never in public. Everyone has a pair and would quite happily spend the rest of their days in them!

- **Baggrundshygge:** background hygge refers to noises heard in the background that evoke a hygge feeling – birds singing, a fire crackling, soft music, people chatting, kids laughing and playing, etc.

- **Hyggeonkel:** the hygge uncle, a person who spends time with the kids, spoiling them and letting them get away with anything – within reason.

- **Hyggetante:** the aunty version of above.

- **Hyggekryds:** relaxing by doing your favorite crossword puzzle.

- **Hyggebamse:** hygge teddy, your favorite stuffed bear that gives you a ton of pleasure.
- **Vovshygge:** dog hygge, when you spend hygge time with your furry pal and if anyone knows how to Hygge naturally, it's a dog.
- **Katthygge:** as above, but with your cat.
- **Hyggesnakkede**: hygge talk, when you have an amazing conversation with your family and friends – more than casual chat and nothing controversial, such as politics.

Classic Danish Hygge Phrases

Along with words, you'll want to learn a few hygge-related phrases, too, so try to learn these. If you ever have the honor of being invited to a Scandinavian hygge event, your hosts will love you for being able to say them:

- **Hvor bor I hyggelist:** If a Scandinavian invites you to their home for the first time, you should say this to them. It's a compliment, and they love to hear it.
- **Tak for en hyggelig aften:** After an evening out or at a friend's house, say this to thank them for a great evening and say goodbye to them.
- **Hyg dig!**: Say this to a friend and you'll be telling

them to have a hyggelig – fun or lovely – time.

- **Uhyggelig:** This has the polar opposite meaning of hyggelig and is used to describe something scary or frightening – Halloween, for example.
- **Hyggesokker:** Sokker means "socks," and the two words combined describe a day or evening at home when all you want to do is put on your cozy socks, curl up, and do nothing – or read or watch a movie, whatever takes your fancy.

And to finish this section, there's a word that describes an overdose of Hygge – hygenygge. It means "intense el. ovedreven hygge" or an intense or overexaggerated type of hygge.

Other Danish Phrases:

A few other Danish phrases that might come in handy and can be used to talk about Hygge are:

Pyt:

Pronounced "pid," this is a concept that is typically used to infer that something is not important. It translates as "Don't worry about it" or "Never mind," but this doesn't really get its truly positive meaning across.

Pyt is more about cultivating a healthy mind and thoughts but is also a common reaction to frustration, errors, or inconvenience. It's also a way that Scandinavian children are taught that nothing is perfect and how to cope with minor setbacks.

Scandinavians also use Pyt to mean "happiness," and one of the most important parts of it is to learn to step back and let your soul and mind reset – a critical part of Hygge.

Umage:

Pronounced "oo-may," this word means to put the effort in to make another person happy. It could be in your job, home, or relationships with loved ones. Umage's essence is in using your inner strength to help another person have a great experience.

It doesn't matter where you are – at home, work, or out shopping. Getting into a routine is too easy, and when something isn't going as well as it should be, it's too easy to shrug your shoulders and say, "That will do." Umage means going further to be the best you can be, not just for yourself but for others.

Overskud:

Pronounced "owa-skood," this word literally translates as "surplus." However, when you use it as a description of a person, it means they have the headspace, energy, and capacity to achieve amazing things. When your mind and body are healthy, and you are motivated to make an effort, achieving overskud is easier. Conversely, the word is also used to describe people who cannot tackle a specific obligation or task. For example, if a Scandinavian person is too busy to attend a social event, they might say they have insufficient "overskud" to go. In simple terms, while something might sound fun, and you really want to go, you simply don't have the energy.

Samfundssind:

Roughly translated, this means "community-mindedness." It comprises two words – samfund, which means society, and ssind, which means mind, and is used as a compound noun. Scandinavian people like to be close to one another, part of a community, and do things together. This is hygge – when you volunteer to do something with other people in your community or get involved in events or anything else that requires people to come together.

Lege and Spille:

Lege has several meanings, but typically, it is used to describe playing with little to no rules, which means your creativity comes into play. Pronounced "layg," it is not the same as another word, "spille," which references playing games or instruments. Everyone needs playtime, even adults, and research shows that letting go and enjoying yourself is great for reducing boredom, fatigue, and stress and increasing well-being. It also allows people to connect to their surroundings and other people. Simply put, make time to enjoy yourself and get together with others to let go of your stress.

Tanemmelighed:

This word comes from "gratus," a Latin word for pleasing or thankfulness, and it is used in hygge terms to mean gratitude. Gratitude is essential to health and well-being, and practicing it regularly can change how you see the world. It can also help knock down stress levels, increase optimism, and even aid better sleep. Celebrate everything in life you have to be thankful for, even the smallest things, so long as they make you happy. Show gratitude whenever possible; if necessary, do it in a journal or send family and friends "thank you" cards. You could even get together with a couple of friends and agree to send each other an email or text every night listing a few things you are grateful for.

These words and phrases can help you live a more fulfilling, happier, healthier life, especially when you take part in Hygge. It is all about the small things that bring you pleasure, the simple things, like a coffee with your friends, a night in with a good book, or anything that makes you happy, so long as it allows you to connect with yourself or others and disconnect from stress and anything else that drags you down.

Conclusion

"It was sunsets that taught me that beauty sometimes only lasts for a couple of moments, and it was sunrises that showed me that all it takes is patience to experience it all over again."
– A.J. Lawless.

That phrase, right there, sums up the beauty of Hygge. It tells you that bringing Hygge into your life is easy, because you don't need to put in much work. Just learn to appreciate the little things in life, the simple things that bring you pleasure. Share your life with others, get together and have fun, and forget everything that makes you anxious, worried, or stressed, if only for a few hours.

You don't have to go all in, either. With Hygge, you can start slow. Do one thing, and when you see how good it makes you feel, add something else. Before you know it, your whole life will be full of Hygge, and you'll be amazed at how carefree, healthy, and happy you feel. The Hygge lifestyle is all about embracing contentment, togetherness, and coziness, creating the perfect safe space for you to be yourself and to be truly happy. Start your Hygge journey right now and discover how great it makes you feel.

References

"3 Steps to Doing Real Hygge -." *All Things Nordic*, 24 Apr. 2019, allthingsnordic.eu/3-steps-to-doing-real-hygge/.

Everygirl, The. "What Happens When You Add a Little Hygge to How You Eat." *The Everygirl*, 11 Nov. 2021, theeverygirl.com/hygge-food/.

"How to Dress Hygge: Your Guide to Bringing the Danish Art of Cozy into Your Wardrobe." *Cate Kittlitz*, catekittlitz.ca/blog/how-to-dress-hygge.

How to Host a Hygge Party. www.pastemagazine.com/food/hygge/hygge-party.

How to Hygge Your Home in 2023: Tips & Tricks for a Cosy Home | Virginia Hayward. 15 Sept. 2023, www.virginiahayward.com/hamperblog/how-to-hygge-your-home-in-2023

Hygge for the Holidays. thedanishway.com/hygge-for-the-holidays/.

"Hygge Your Way to Productivity: 10 Danish Words to Elevate Your Workplace." *Calendar*, 28 Dec. 2023, www.calendar.com/blog/hygge-your-way-to-productivity-10-danish-words-to-elevate-your-workplace-and-life/.

"Hygge-Fy Your Relationships: Create Warmth, Comfort, and Intimacy in Your Life." *Alexandria Stylebook*, alexandriastylebook.com/alexandria-stylebook/hygge-fy-your-relationships-create-warmth-comfort-and-intimacy-in-your-life-delraypsychandwellness-january-2022.

ingebretsens. "Hygge Vocabulary." *Ingebretsen's Nordic Marketplace*, 6 Jan. 2018, ingebretsens-blog.com/hygge-vocabulary/.

Therapy, My Online. "What Is "Hygge" and Why Is It Good for Mental Health?" *My Online Therapy*, 25 Feb. 2022, myonlinetherapy.com/what-is-hygge-and-why-is-it-good-for-mental-health/.